GEMS OF HABIT

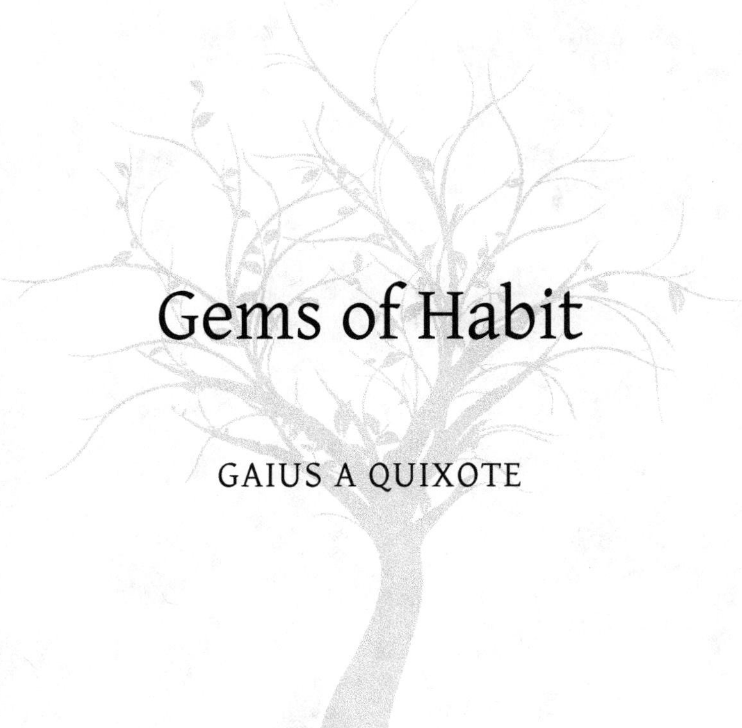

Gems of Habit

GAIUS A QUIXOTE

Gaius A Quixote

Cover art by Ariel

First printing, 2020

ISBN: 9781735573007

Gaius A Quixote
P.O. Box 2431
797 Sam Bass Rd, Round Rock, TX
78680

Gaius.a.q@gmail.com

TABLE OF CONTENTS

1

A Quiet Time

People of the weekend are a lonely people
But you are a person of the week

Each day a plod?
In time, you'll be seasoned
And this silence
Will build roots

As others ache for noise
You build a road
Of solid thought
And gain the only joy

2

The boy laughs louder as each day passes.
His voice grows louder, and his ears hear less.
His touch of hands now rough and firm.

3

From a Good Parent
Gems of habits crafted over years
Take care of habits easily lost—
Polish daily
For luster lost is corrosive
Gems of others mixed, confuse habits prized
Building most prized
Only through decades of scrutiny

4

Morning sun sending shivers
As nighttime gloom grooms careless impulse

Dawn is a thief
As dusk is adrift

Awake! Awake
There's work to do

Say a prayer
And smile past both

5

To the mother
Teaching meaningful apologies
Showing that burdens are good
And resolving worries
With simple words and prayer

6

Men with open windows
Always on guard

You are the cool breeze of Fall
You are the Winter

Keep your soul
The guests are here
A change is coming

7

To a shadow I speak
A lonely apparition
This stranger

Never again will his face appear

"You're beautiful," he said.
As she turned away

Oh that sand I laid in pulls me under
I go there some nights and tell him I know
I tell him I'm not angry

8

"You're different,"
A friend said
"What made you so?"

Allowing that shiny polish
From mother's womb
The residue that numbs,
That glazes eyes
To rub off

For frail life within cocoon
Lasts as long as impetus is vacant
That driving force that must express
That must impress

9

An evening breeze
A summoning of that red hall
Once felt in youth

Staring at this grand hall

Walls a hundred feet tall
In reverence to these people
With clothes of plastic
Reflecting cast of light

10

Passing Glance
A smiling face
Guarding gloom

For showing withered stem
Thrills lawless impulse

Oh flowing stream,
Bounded by these creases;
Open chasms
In this weathered mound

Elders; gray hairs and grace
Intrigues the young
As finger streaks in dust

All made light
By hanging ornaments and rouge
Their partner

From playful fingers
Applied till
Whim is met

11

Thorn in my foot
This fever inside

To vice I go
For freedom

But this grip within
Is tighter, now

12

The Theater
Golden doors and red carpet
I squint at lights inside

Fizzing drinks
Sprinkling sticky hands
Children hopping
Spilling popcorn

Smiling faces in rows we sit
As event begins
Lights turn off
Past nuisances now wriggling away

Perfect faces flashing on the screen
We can't compare
In beauty or wit.

Us strangers
In this booming den

Obedient we sit

As lights turn on
To an empty room

13

Happy glow
What keeps is habit

Never wait my friends
Eschew dull eyes
Culling stream of gold

Weak soil surrounds
Scaffolding's buttress
Is determination

Once vein of bright is found
Fixed eyes only
Never losing sight

A king's substance within

No patch on shoulder
Or medal on breast

All else fails
But this crown I wear

14

Anchored
Swaying vessel
For spray of life
A groaning
For that clinking upward

These links of chain
Latched to rock below

Dark waves
Those waves
Of churning power
Where is that mirage,
That vast expanse?

A light below
From inside window
A captain sits

To cry,
That pure concession
Of this slave to wind

This face this wooden mask
Looking through glass for cracks and scars
Though none are found

Those eyes,
Echoes of concern

That weariness will turn

A sternness
Bristling at every mirror
To break outside
As inward chamber is

15

Too Many
Voices let in today
Regime of mine they cast away

Circling friends
These hopes of mine

The brook now gone
Had flowed to me

16

Old Words

Within spells A mystic craft
From ink
Now hammered
Etched in soft wooded blankets

Each word opaque
Till the vessel
Open and transparent
A crack even leaves room
For sprouting seed

The mystic roots now taken hold
Where past brushes on this tun remain
Time enough for Pan
His green moss laying rest

Adding color to this once plain vat
Now weather alter,
From Gia's opened palm

17

Far from bed
Late at night
Shifting thoughts behind red eyes

Hallways walked
Doors doors
Snoring behind closed doors

Till in basement
Things are quiet
Big names, distracting thoughts

He's not waiting
His mind is working
Working thoughts
To hush that growl

18

To be a boy
Is to throw rocks
Jab sticks,
Smash teeth
And break windows

To be a boy
Is to read little and pick weeds
Run through fields through muddy trails
Climb trees and wrestle near bonfires

To be a boy is to
Sit by girls in quiet joy
To ache for stars and smoky tents

To be a boy again
Is not knowing when to stop

19

Stored Oats
Oath to self
A stirring within
A course is set

Till door left often
What then was stored
Now blows away

20

Nubile
Look to her!
Young and full of life
Cherish her innocence that mirrors heaven

Energy springs from a well and it won't stop!
Her neighbors to South call on her door

Just as Eastern books emphasize,
And our fathers trifled with as kids; breathe

Leviathan is here
Its arms taking us into cloaca
Holding us at all hours of day
The only remedy is towards an ideal

We see stars alike
What differs is fancy device
This device when too complex cuts
Before Occam does his job

Let us end this sardonic thread
Which has turned acidic
Let us weave a beautiful thread
Binding us together as we gaze to heaven after work

Oh that work is more inward than outward
I told mother my heart aches for pulling weeds

No country compares

To this devil that drives

Musk, he moves arteries in ground
He stirs hearts of young with
Dreams of pilgrimage

This buzz this zap
This pounding in heart This is home.

21

The Bachelor

Among fog and skeptics
A bachelor in the night

Staring at palm and fingers
A star shines
In puddle at foot

He looks to star
And meditates
A flower is sprouting
The night of wandering ends

Lighting a candle and
Saying a prayer
He drinks with spirits
At close of night

22

Artifex

Some potters
Less crafty than others
Still do make

For make they must or fore last breath
In cold will see
Their shadow sink to dust

23

This body is not mine
Though do I try and make it so
Through draping dress and tight clothes

Dark colors of serious days
The hair on top may change so, too

I do know
This body is not mine
Though do I try and make it so

24

A pond breaks as child jumps
Stirring fish and mud

25

Dear friend, go forward
Pictures and puppets
Has no hold of head

What was garnered
Will last

Till reaching point of
Illusions lost
With ways told how
By marionettes

Forming towards my purpose
If limbs break off
No matter
The mind is hard at work

What has been garnered will last
Outlasting all

26

The Farmer

On porch he sits
Watching loosened earth

A moving grey
Over seed in field

Standing now
He goes inside and

To mirror in room
He speaks to self

27

To my comrade
Who welcomed me

Your character;
An oak in open field

Providing shade
For he who wanders

28

Georgia Warmth of Spring
No friend or lover
Could be this tranquil
So rare and brief

Lowering sun
In quiet air
A Church bell rings

29

Away the smack
Of pictures
Of flashing lights and noise

I leave now
As memories
Send me to an empty room
Inside my home

30

Dancing in my room
I thought alone

Though breathing hard now
I hear his breath in mine

So I breathe quieter,
Quieter now

31
To Victory
It wakes before others
Smiling when others don't

When sullen look besets another
It offers good word

For the day isn't bad
Nor the work there in

32

To you who gives kind words
A light to corners end
An acquaintance brief
Though a friend nonetheless

So thank you.
That pat on back, you gave.
Brief moment
But staving off that grubby hand that tries,
Oh it tries, pulling good under
But you who offers kind words, you who gives,
I salute

Inner know-it-all says,
"Good words given are bad for ego."
I say, as lion-pride, use your pride for confidence
And gather you and friends.

Oh the deconstructionist
Tearing everything; saying pride is bad,
Saying all ego is bad
“Eradicate and start over,” he says

Perhaps a dirty spot within he tries erase
So much erased that little buttress remains

And now you have nothing but scaffolding
Over half a thought

But when people still have pride
They tower,
Blackening sky

For they take all light and all heat
While those in shade
Find little warmth or growth

33

An afterthought
My friend,
This is new.
Strange customs and tasks
Don't hurt yourself with mean look

If others aren't kind, though often they are
Allow kindness to self.
This job can be done!

When told to go, go and do
When asked a question
Answer and act
This task, an adventure.

Look not alone to foreign lands
With strange sounds in mouths
Wrong my friend.
Though lands abroad are grand
And travelling them is encouraged

I say, do not overlook
Adventure of taking task on self
Of embracing confidence
This confidence, a friend to adventure

Oh friend,
Please do away with the drudge, arresting spirit
Pulling thoughts down toward failure

In each moment of stress and uncertainty
A battle within;
A grand adventure!
Enough of desperation

You leader of self
People will see and call on you
In moments of stress, see yourself
You will continue forward.

You have traveled this path a hundred times
But this time, you won't overlook,
Taking blindness through words in duress.

Away with narrow view of happiness,
That image of mansion,
Of shiny car and trendy looks

Oh the hollow that holler,
That deep valley is no place for pose of fight
Though once down there, heel dug in,
Being no choice, do dig in

A game, a sport is the goal
what growth beyond, come what may
And this growth beyond will come.
Allow it.
Often arriving as smiling face or firm handshake.

What a game!

A full team you have within
Do not neglect each player
This game, this back and forth at play

Rolling waves within
Powerful waves that must be watched
Just as storms are watched for

Inside self is trivialized only till motion is too fast
Is too much that one cannot contain
Then reckless lashes
Decisions a whim.

Had gentle care been taken to that frail moment
That running back to boss for help
When full course had not gone through
When all extremities had not been explored
Those moments my friend, why trivialize them?

Yes, among the mundane,
The usual the non-exciting
But the pulling down
The giving up
And too often demeaning of self

Like all others there is a great inside.
You fear others? You respect others?
The king within you holds the power.
Respect his power
You're done overlooking this man

34

Echoes from Self: A Soliloquy

It’s all relative I say
Often times difference is
One who forgets all else but craft
And the one dissatisfied in day

All struggle alike
But some peak over
While others remain stuck behind.
All battles alike

Do not compare for envy corrupts.
Look to past self in yesterday
See improvement; see backwards step
Make change or hold a course

There is likeness within
Shared motifs
Use this knowing
To bond that which outside separates

35

Brother and sister
Why drop your bucket in a well
That you know has bad water?

Look! The frail artist who lies in gutter

To the man who has capital but
Won't spend toward a
Comfy couch for future guests
Who won't buy art for pale wall

Keeping rooms bland
No character but plain plain plain
"I want a simple life," he says

Such wishes such wants
Oh you humble sir
Is that your goal?

What's in you?
A grandness to share with world?
Or a man shrinking in corner?

This humble figure
This simple picture made from putty.
This man once before had shape
This boy once before had character

36

At First Sight
Your course is set
Though funny sad is
Myopic young age
Through knee jerk
And sharp comments
Show more truth in action
Than old age in words

37

A Statue
Allowing soul a mirror
A picture of Father
In time of strength
That gift
That is solace
When times of
Bad moves aside
And peace ensues
That is victory
No need to drain the coffer
Or huff the smoke

CPSIA information can be obtained
at www.ICGtesting.com
Printed in the USA
LVHW081639230920
666052LV00054B/537

9 781735 573007